Profits via ETFs

Tony Pow

Why you invest

You need to learn about investing sooner or later in your life. You need to take some calculated risks.

Compare the returns of the following assets: cash, CDs, treasury bills, bonds, real estate and stocks. We start with the risk-free investments and end with the riskiest. It turns out that the average returns are in the opposite order. Cash and CDs are not risk-free as inflation eats our profits. For example, the real return is negative for the 2% return in a CD and a 3% inflation rate. In addition you have to pay taxes for the 'returns'. Our capitalist system punishes us for not taking risk.

There are two kinds of risk: blind risk and calculated risk. If you buy a stock due to a recommendation from a commentator on TV or a tip, most likely you are taking a blind risk. It would be the same in buying a house without thoroughly evaluating the house and its neighborhood. When you buy stocks with a proven strategy (i.e. when/what stocks to buy and when/what stocks to sell), you are taking a calculated risk. In the long run, stocks with calculated and educated risks are profitable.

Be a turtle investor by investing in value stocks and holding for longer time periods (a year or more). "Buy and Monitor" is better an approach than "Buy and Hold" as some could lose all the stock values such as in the failure of Enron.

For experienced investors, shorting, short-term trading and covered calls would make you good profits. Simple market timing would reduce your losses during market down turns. If you buy a market ETF and use my simple market timing, you should have beaten the market by a wide margin from 2000 to 2019.

With so many frauds and poor management, do not trust anyone with your investing. Do not buy investing instruments that are highly marketed such as annuity and term insurance.

If you are a handy man and do not mind to satisfy the constant requests of your tenants, buy real estate in growing areas could be very profitable in the long run.Take advantage of the tax laws such as investing in a 401K especially the part that is matched by your company and/or a Roth IRA.

Why you want to read this book

It should improve your financial health substantially. There are about a million investment books. Why we need another one?

- I select proven ideas from more than 100 books besides my original ideas and experiences. I also include links to current articles that will bring more depth to the topic. It is not a novel or documenting the story of my life. All related chapters are grouped in a section for easy future reference. Some chapters are not easy to digest as they have a lot of pointers and some may require you to try them out yourself.

- A best seller was written by a young writer whose main income was from his books and none from his investing. His book is good for beginners or you want to brush up your English. Most of my incomes are from investing.

- Many popular books claiming the authors making millions. However, usually their techniques are hard to follow. Many admitted they had been bankrupted many times. Hence, their chance of bankrupting again is very high. Is bankruptcy fine with you? I cannot afford bankruptcy past and present. My techniques minimize risking my money.

- There are many popular books. They worked very well at one time and folks making millions following the advice. However, look at their recent performances of the last five years. Most of them cannot even beat the S&P 500 index.

- Check the recent mediocre performance of gurus such as Buffett. They are the market and they cannot beat themselves. Their techniques may no longer work.

- As of this writing (10/2017), I do not know any reviewers on my books in Amazon.com and I have donated all my profits from my books to charities.

Contents

Filler

I got a call from Buffett asking me to lead their stock research.
I asked him why for a nobody; you may be asking the same question.
No kidding.

He told me that he should have read my book Scoring Stocks to buy Apple instead of IBM in May, 2013. It would save his company millions of dollars minus $10 for my book. Not to mention the market timing technique that had worked in the last two major market plunges.

I told him, "OK, I'll beat your mediocre returns of the last 5 years."
He said, "You can do better than that and at least beat SPY. If you do so, no one will be that stupid to leave my fund and pay the hefty capital gain taxes."

I told him, "I cannot beat the market as you are the market especially after your expensive fees. In addition, I do not know how to avoid day traders from riding my wagon in trading. Also most of my big profits were made in small stocks that your fund cannot trade besides owning the company."

I woke up trembling. I'm glad it is only a nightmare
--
Joke, reality or just nightmare, you decide.

Introduction

Investing could be simple and profitable to beginners and experts alike. The best and easiest way is using ETFs. Most fund managers and hedge fund managers after their hefty fees cannot beat the market index. Just buy SPY (an ETF simulating the market) and you're diversified and most likely beat most fund managers.

This book is different from most other books on this topic. There are many techniques hidden that help you to beat the market and at the same time ensure safety for your hard-earned money.

The average of the loss of the last two market crashes is about 45% from their peaks. It is the main theme in this book and I allocate a good portion of this book to simple market timing. I also debunk the myth of "you cannot time the market". There may be false signals but they correct themselves shortly.

I use the simplest way to time the market without the hard-to-learn charting. Just follow the simple techniques. There is nothing else besides this low-priced book to buy or subscribe.

This book describes the examples and my experiences of exiting the market to reduce your losses and reentering the market for the best profits. I made 80% in my largest taxable account in 2009.

Selling stocks and buying stocks take a lot of time and emotions vs. trading ETFs. I also provide a simple way to evaluate ETFs using free information in the web.

When the signal tells us to buy, you can profit by buying any ETF that simulates the market. ETF rotation could make you even more profit. It is described in this book.

How this book is organized

Most graphs are in landscape orientation for both paperback and e-readers. Some graphs may not be displayed adequately on a small screen of an e-reader. E-readers may be available in the current version of Windows, so you can read e-books on the larger screen of your PC. For better orientation, just flip the e-readers 90 degrees.

A link is usually included for these screens. Copy it to your browser to display the graphs on your PC if desirable. Instructions on how to produce some graphs are provided as you should try them out. One example is how to produce a chart on detecting market crashes.

It is easier to display some tables in landscape mode, which can be selected in your e-reader. Select a table or a graph via your e-reader to display it to fit the screen.

The font size and page size of most e-book formats can be adjusted. The unknown, special character is the "smiling face" that the current Kindle does not convert correctly.

There are clickable links to web articles. Most of them are from my own web sites and public web sites such as Wikipedia. Some public links may not be available in the future as they are not under my control.

Fidelity Video provides video clips to explain some basic terms and it may require Fidelity customers to sign on in order to view them. Check the trial offer from Fidelity. YouTube offers similar video lessons.

These links extend the usefulness of this book by making available specific topics that may not be interesting to every reader.

The current version provides most of the links the paperback readers can enter into your browser. Get the same information by entering a search in Wikipedia such as Dogs of Dow.

Investopedia is another source beside Wikipedia.

http://www.investopedia.com/

'Afterthoughts' includes my additional comments and comments from others. Readers can make comments in this book's website. These comments may be included in the Afterthoughts in subsequent revisions, with the commenter's last name redacted. It is the section of the article for freer and informal discussion.

There are fillers with tips and jokes to fill up the empty space of the printed book.

For convenience, this book uses SPY, an Exchange Traded Fund (ETF) simulating the S&P 500 index, as the benchmark for the market.

Annualized returns (Return * 365 / (Days between)) are used where appropriate for more meaningful comparison. To illustrate, I have a 10% return in 6 months, a 10% in a year and a 10% in 2 years. It is more meaningful to use annualized returns of 20%, 10% and 5% respectively for the 6-month return, the one-year return and the 2-year return in this example.

Usually I do not include the dividend, so you can add an estimated 1.5% to the annualized return. In addition, compound interest is not used for easier calculation, so the actual return could be even better.

About the author

I graduated from Cal. State University at San Jose in Industrial Engineering and University of Mass. in Amherst with a MS in Industrial Engineering. I have retired from a job in IT. I have been an investor for over 30 years.

My articles in SeekingAlpha.com.
Click the link (http://seekingalpha.com/author/tony-pow/articles).

Dedication

To all retail investors and future retail investors including my grandchildren.

Acknowledgement

Thanks to Seeking Alpha, Wikipedia and Investopedia for the many helpful links to enrich this book. Yahoo!Finance and Finviz.com for the tools and charts used in this book.

Important notices

Version	Paperback	Kindle
1.0	09/15	09/15
1.4	02/16	04/16
2.0	10/19	10/19
2.2	01/21	01/21

Printed version. ISBN-13: 978-1517297688 ISBN-10: 1517297680

Book store managers can order the printed books from Createspace.com.
https://tonyp4idea.blogspot.com/2020/12/book-managers.html

Book update.
https://ebmyth.blogspot.com/2020/12/updates-for-all-books.html

If you believe this book is beneficial, please comment in Amazon.com or similar sites and imagine how "Complete the art of investment (Kindle version has about 850 6*9 pages)" would benefit you financially.

Disclaimer

market conditions and /or your individual situations. The values of some parameters such as RSI(14) are arbitrarily set by me. My publisher and I are not liable for any damages in using this book or its contents.

If you are reading my concise version (100 pages or less) and find it useful, you may want to check out "Complete the art of investing" which has over 850 pages (Kindle version).

Section I: ETF & resources

1   ETFs / Mutual Funds

What is an ETF

Fidelity: Index ETFs (https://www.fidelity.com/etfs/overview).

Wikipedia on ETF (http://en.wikipedia.org/wiki/Exchange-traded_fund).

List of ETFs
ETF Bloomberg
http://www.bloomberg.com/markets/etfs/
ETF data base
http://etfdb.com/
ETF Trends
http://www.etftrends.com/
A list of ETFs. Seeking Alpha.
(http://etf.stock-encyclopedia.com/category/)

Fidelity's commission-free ETFs. Check current offerings and whether they are still commission-free.
(https://www.fidelity.com/etfs/ishares)

Fidelity Annuity funds with performance data.
http://fundresearch.fidelity.com/annuities/category-performance-annual-total-returns-quarterly/FPRAI?refann=005

A list of contra ETFs (or bear ETFs)
http://www.tradermike.net/inverse-short-etfs-bearish-etf-funds/

Misc.: ETFGuide, ETFReplay (highly recommended).

Other resources
Your broker should have a lot of information on ETFs and many offer commission-free ETFs.

Most subscription services offer research on ETFs. IBD has a strategy dedicated to ETFs and so does AAII to name a couple.

Seeking Alpha has extensive resources for ETF including an ETF screener and investing ideas.

Not all ETFs are created equal
Check their performances and their expenses.

Small but well-performing ETFs
Here is a list.
http://finance.yahoo.com/news/small-etfs-pack-big-punch-195430875.html

Guggenheim Spin-Off ETF (CSD) looks interesting. The ETF tracks corporate spinoffs. It has beaten SPY for a long time; check the current performance. Not a recommendation.

When not to use ETFs
I prefer sector mutual funds in some industries but you need to do extensive research. They are drug industry, banks, miners and insurers.

Half ETF
Taking out half of the stocks that score below the average in an index ETF could beat the same full ETF itself. I call it HETF (half the ETF). You heard it here first.

To illustrate, sort the expected P/E (not including stocks with negative earnings) in ascending order and only include the stocks on the first half. Add more fundamental metrics. It will take a few minutes.

Disadvantages of ETFs

- When you have two stocks in a sector ETF one good one and one bad one, the ETF treats them the same. Stock pickers would buy the one that has a better appreciation potential.

- The return is better than the actual return due to stock rotation. To illustrate this, on August 29, 2012, SHLD was replaced by LYB in a sector fund. SHLD was down by 4% and LYB was up by 4% primarily due to the switch. Unless you sell and buy at the right time (which is impossible), your return would not match the ETF's returns due to the replacement.
- Ensure the performance matches the corresponding index, but will most likely not include dividends.

Advantages of ETFs

- We have demonstrated that you can beat the market by using market timing. Between 2000 and Nov., 2013, you only exit and reenter the market 3 times and the result is astonishing.
- It is easy to rotate a sector vs. buying/selling all of the stocks in this sector. It makes sector rotation the same as trading a stock.
- The risk is spread out and your portfolio is diversified especially for a market ETF or buying three or more ETFs in different sectors.
- Eliminate the time in researching stocks.

Leveraged ETFs

I do not recommend them. Some are 2x, 3x and even higher. They're too risky. However, when you are very sure or your tested strategy has very low drawdown, you may want to use them to improve performance. I recommend skipping all leveraged ETFs.

My basic ETF tables

I use a list of selected ETFs and commission-free (check the details) ETFs from Fidelity for my purpose. I include some mutual funds in Fidelity's annuity. Some of these may be interesting to you. I use ETFs for sector rotation and parking my cash when the market is favorable and I do not have stocks that I want to buy.

ETFs and funds come and go. Some ideas and classifications are my own interpretation.

Table by market cap:

Category	ETF	Fidelity ETF	Mutual Funds	Fidelity's Annuity	Contra ETF
Size:					
Large Cap	DIA		See Blend		DOG
	SPY				SH
	QQQ	ONEQ			PSQ
	RYH				
Blend	IWD	IVV	BEQGX		
Growth	SPYG	IVW	FBGRX		
Value	SPYV		DOGGX		
Dividend	NOBL	DVY	FRDPX		
	VYM				
Mid Cap				FNBSC	MYY
Blend	MDY	JJH	VSEQX		
Growth		IJK	STDIX		
			BPTRX		
Value		IJJ	FSMVX		
Small Cap				FPRGC	SBB
Blend	IWM	IJR	HDPSX		
Growth		IJT	PRDSX		
Value		IJS	SKSEX		
Micro	IWC				
Multi					
Blend			VDEOX		
Growth			VHCOX		
Value			TCLCX		
Bond					
Long Term (20)	VLV		BTTTX		TBF
Mid Term (7 – 10)	VCIT		FSTGX		
Short Term (1 – 3 yrs.)	VCSH		THOPX		
Total	BOND		PONDX		
Corp Invest Grade	VCIT		NTHEX		
High Yield (junk)	PHB		SPHIX		
Muni	MUB		Check state		

Table by sectors:

Sector	ETF	Fidelity ETF	Mutual Funds	Fidelity's Annuity
Banking[1]			FSRBK	
Regional	IAT			
Bio Tech	IBB		FBIOX	
	XBI		Large	
Consumer Dis.	XLY	FDIS	FSCPX	FVHAC
Consumer Staple	XLP	FSTA	FDFAX	FCSAC
Finance	KIE	FNCL	FIDSX	FONNC
	IYF			
Energy	XLE	FENY	FSENX	FJLLC
Energy Service			FSESX	
Gold	GLD		FSAGX	
Gold Miner	GDX		VGPMX	
Health Care	IYH	FHLC	FSPHX	FPDRC
	VHT		VGHCX	
House Builder	ITB		FSHOX	
	ITB		Perform	
Industrial	IYJ	FIDU	FCYIX	FBALC
Material	VAW	FMAT	FSDPX	
	IYM			
Oil	USO			
Oil Service	OIH		FSESX	
Oil Exploration	XOP			
Real Estate	VNQ		FRIFX	FFWLC
REIT	VNQ			
Retail	RTH		FSRPX	
	XRT			
Regional bank	KRE		FSRBX	
Semi Conduct	SMH			
Software	XSW		FSCSX	
	IGV			
Technology	XLK	FTEC	FSPTX	FYENC
	FDN		FBSOX	
Telecomm.	VOX	FCOM	FSTCX	FVTAC
Transport	XTN			
	IYT			
Utilities	XLU	FUTY	FSUTX	FKMSC
Wireless			FWRLX	

Table by countries outside the USA:

Country	ETF	Fidelity ETF	Mutual Funds	Fidelity's Annuity
Australia	EWA			
Brazil	EWZ			
Canada	EWC		FICDX	
China	FXI		FHKCX	
EAFE	EFA			
Emerging	VWO		FEMEX	FEMAC
Europe	VGK		FIEUX	
Global	KXI		PGVFX	
Greece	GREK			
India	INDY		MINDX	
Indonesia	EIDO			
Latin America	ILF		FLATX	
Nordic			FNORX	
Hong Kong	EWH			
Japan	EWJ		FJPNX	
S. Africa	EZA			
S. Korea	EWY		MAKOX	
Singapore	EWS			
Taiwan	EWT			
	TUR			
United Kingdom	EWU			
Foreign:				
Combination	1	2	3	4
Intern. Div.	IDV	DWX		
Small Cap	SCZ	GWX		
Value	EFV			
Europe	VGK			

Free sites for ETFs

ETFReplay is great for testing but not free. There are many good free sites for ETFs. I describe Seeking Alpha, ETFdb and Finviz here. They have duplicated features and I only include features that are unique and/or I use them myself. With these three sites you should get most info on ETFs.

Seeking Alpha

Seeking Alpha is an investing site. From Home, select "ETFs and Funds". There are many current articles on ETFs. ETF Guide is excellent for beginners.

ETF Screener. My favorite search is "1-month > 5%" and "market cap > 100M".

ETFdb

It is quite complete for research for the full version. Enter a symbol of ETF and it displays all the information about it. This is the only site I know that has the P/E of an ETF – Yahoo!Finance used to have this info.

Finviz

Still some info are not readily available from the above two sites. The next one I use most is Finviz for YTD performance (and other performances), dividend %, avg. volume, SMA-20%, SMA-50%, SMA-200%, short ratio and RSI(14) in addition to the chart.

#Fillers: I wish I have a time machine

After collecting bottles for money, an old lady ordered a bowl of plain rice and ate by herself. I wish I could have ordered a meat dish for her as I was 'ashamed' of being generous.

A well-dressed gentleman offered his just-bought hamburger to a beggar. The beggar refused and asked for money instead – most likely he needed the money to buy liquor. A tale of two citizens.

During a lunch with my fellow tourists, a beautiful girl danced for our entertainment. I did not offer her anything and it had been bothering me for years.

During college, my housemates asked me to apply for food stamps. I had used only a few stamps then as I did not cook. I feel ashamed as this is my only time to collect social welfare.

We have regrets in life and we can only bring them to our graves.

If I have a time machine, I would win the lottery. LOL.

2 Quick analysis of ETFs

Evaluate an ETF

ETFs are a basket of stocks according to the market, a specific sector, country or a specific theme.

Yahoo!Finance used to give the P/E of an ETF. Try to get it from ETFdb.com. Enter the symbol of the ETF such as XLU, and then select Valuation. If it is below 15 and above zero, it could be a value ETF. Also, if the current price is lower than its NAV, it is sold at a discount (or premium vice versa). Compare its YTD Return to SPY's.

Alternatively, get similar info from http://www.multpl.com/. In addition, this web site provides the following metrics: Shiller P/E, Price/Sales, and Price/Book.

From Finviz.com, enter the ETF symbol. If SMA-20%, SMA-50% and SMA-200% are all positive, most likely the ETF is in an uptrend. To illustrate, SMA-200 is Simple Moving Average for the last 200 trading sessions (no trading on weekends and specific holidays). The percent is how much the stock price of the ETF is above the SMA. If the percent is negative, it means the stock price is below the SMA.

If your average holding period of your stocks is about 50 days, SMA-50% is more appropriate to you.

If RSI(14) > 70, it is probably over-sold; if it is < 35, it is probably under-sold (indicating value).

In addition, ensure the ETF's average volume is high (I suggest more than 10,000 shares), the market cap is more than 300 M, and it has low fees. Most popular ETFs have these characteristics. Beginners should avoid leveraged ETFs.

How to determine if the sector has been recovered

It is easier to profit by following the uptrend of an ETF using the above info. It is hard to detect when the bottom of an ETF has been reached. If SMA-20%, SMA-50% and SMA-200% are all positive, most likely the ETF is in an uptrend or it has recovered. It does not always happen as predicted, so use stops to protect your investment.

An example
First, determine whether the market is risky. Most beginners should not invest in a risky market. Advanced investors can bet against the market or a specific sector by buying contra ETFs or puts.

Next, you want to limit the number of sector ETFs by selecting those that are either in an uptrend or hitting bottom (bottom is hard to predict). Personally I prefer sectors with long-term uptrends (indicated by articles found in many web sites including cnnfn.com and Seeking Alpha.

For illustration purposes only for deteriorating market conditions, I would select the following ETFs: SPY (simulating the market based on large companies) and XLP (consumer staples). XLP should perform better than XLY (consumer discretionary) during a recession as those products are the necessities.

Technical indicators such as SMA-50 (Simple Moving Average for the last 50 sessions), SMA-200 and RSI(14) are obtained from Finviz.com and the rest are obtained from Yahoo!Finance.com. After you buy the ETF, use a stop loss to protect your investment. For example, bio tech sector moved up for many months until it crashed in 2015. Change the stop loss value every month to protect your gains in this case.

As of 2/5/2016	SPY	XLP (Staples)	XLY (Discret.)
Price	190	50	71
NAV	192	50	73
• Technical			
SMA-50	-4%	0%	-7%
SMA-200	-6%	2%	-7%
RSI(14)	44	50	36
Other	Double bottom at $186		
• Fundamental			
P/E	17	20	19
Yield	2.1%	2.5%	1.5%
YTD return	-5%	0.5%	-5%
Net asset	174 B	9 B	10 B

Explanation

- The figures may not be identical among web sites due to the dates they are using.
- XLY has best discount among the 3 ETFs as most investors believe a recession is coming.
- XLP has less down trend among the 3 ETFs as expected.
- XLY is more undersold among the three as expected.
- Double bottom is a technical pattern that indicates the stock would surge upward.
- SPY has a better value according to its P/E.
- XLY's dividend is the least among the three as they have more tech companies in the ETF. They have to plow back the profits to research and development.
- XLP has the best YTD return among the three.
- As long as the asset is above 500 M (200 M for specialized ETFs), it is fine and all three pass this mark.

There are many metrics such as Debt/Equity not readily available from most web sites. Many sites list the top holdings of a specific ETF. Just average the metrics of the top ten or so of its stock holdings.

3   An example

This example evaluates RING, a gold miner, using ETFdb and Finviz that are free from the web. The data is from July, 6, 2020.

Bring up ETFdb and enter RING in the search. There are basic info that are important to me: Sector (gold miners), Asset Size (Large-Cap), Issuer (iShares), Inception (Jan. 31, 2012), Expense Ratio (0.39%) and Tax Form (1099).

They fit all my requirements. The expense ratio is higher than most ETFs that simulating an index such as SPY. I try to trade ETFs using Tax Form 1099 in my taxable accounts. The large cap created about 8 years ago by a reputable company are good.

Select "Dividend and Valuation". P/E of 17.39 is fine in a rank of 11 in 27 in similar group of ETFs. As in my books, I stated it is hard to evaluate miners. I buy this ETF primarily to fight the possibility of inflation and the potential depreciation of USD. The dividend rate of 0.52% (0.70% from Finviz) is in the low range of the scale; it is fine for me as dividend is not my concern.

There are more info from this web site. For simplicity, bring up Finviz:
- The short-term trend is up (SMA-20% = 8% and SMA-50% = 7%).
- The long-term trend is up (SMA-200% = 26%).
- It is close to overbought (RSI(14) = 64%; 65% to me is overbought).
- It is -4% from 52-w High. It has performed well from the YTD, Last Year, Last Quarter, Last Month and Last Week.
- It almost doubles in price from mid March this year.
- Avg. Vol. is fine.

From ETFdb, check the Holding. It has 39 stocks, so it is quite diversified for this industry. The two top holdings are NEM (19%) and ABX (18%), which is listed as GOLD in NYSX. I also consider to buy these two stocks in addition to RING. You can estimate the other metrics that are not available by averaging these two stocks. Here is my summary:

STOCK	NEM	GOLD
Forward P/E	20	25
Debt / Share	0.31	0.24
ROE	17%	22%
Sales Q/Q	43%	30%
EPS Q/Q	389%	254%
SMA50	2%	4%
RSI(14)	59%	60%
Insider Trans	-13%	N/A
Fidelity's Equity Summary Score	6.1	6.8

4   Rotate four ETFs

We can beat the market by rotating one ETF that represents the market such as SPY and cash (or short-term bond ETF) via market timing.

During a market uptrend, rotating the following four ETFs could be more profitable. Be warned that a short-term capital gain in taxable accounts is not treated as favorably as the long-term capital gain; check current tax laws.

The allocation percentages depend on your individual risk tolerance. You can use indexed mutual funds. Compare their expenses and restrictions. Some mutual funds charge you if you withdraw within a specific time period.

Select the best performer of last month (from Seeking Alpha, cnnFn, or the ETF/mutual fund site). Add a contra ETF such as SH to take advantage of a falling market for more aggressive investors. Add sector ETFs to the four ETFs such as XLY, XLP, XLE, XLF, XLU, IYW, XHB, IYM, OIL and XLU to expand your selection.

ETFs	Money Market	US	International	Bond
Fidelity		Spartan Total Market	Spartan Global Market	Spartan US Bond
Vanguard		Total Stock Market	Total International Market	Total Bond Market
My choice	Fidelity	SPY	Vanguard	Fidelity
Suggest %				
During Market plunge	90%	0%	0%	10%
After plunge	10%	60%	10%	20%

Explanation

- The above are suggestions only. If your broker offers similar ETFs, consider using them.
- Check out any restrictions of the ETFs.
- 4 ETFs (one actually is a money market fund) are enough for most starters. They are diversified, low-cost and you do not need balancing

except during a market plunge (refer to the chapter on Detecting Market Plunges).

- The percentages are suggestions only. If you are less risk tolerant, allocate more to a money market fund, CD and/or bond ETF.
- Have at least 10% allocated to the money market fund. When there is a mild market dip, move the money market fund to the US equity fund. Move it back to money market when there is a mild market upsurge. If you do not have time to check the market, allocate this 10% to the bond ETF.
- When the market is risky, reduce stock equities (i.e. increase money market and bond allocations).
- The symbols for Fidelity ETFs are FSTMX, FSGDX and FBIDX.
- The symbols for Vanguard ETFs are VTSMX, VGTSX and VBMFX.
- If you are more advanced, use additional sector ETFs to rotate. Find out the current winners from many sources including CNNfn.com. Also buy long-term bond funds (such as 30-year Treasury) when the interest rates is 10% or more. I have now covered the basics in sector rotation for you.

Simplest ETF Rotation

This is an abstract from my book ETF Rotation for Couch Potatoes. I recommend the following as a guideline to establish your own portfolio, your own testing and your own strategy.

Common monthly task

1. Detect market timing. If the market is plunging, stay in cash.
2. Check whether the strategy is still working recently. Do it at least once a year.

Best short-term performers (2013-2016)
Performance (using SPY as the benchmark)

Portfolio	CAGR (2 months)	CAGR (20 days)
SPY	8.8%	8.8%
8 –Sector	5.5%	**12.3%**

ETFs included in portfolio

No.	Name	ETFs
8	Sector	GDX, IYF, IYH, KBE, KRE, OIH, RTH, SMH, UNG, USO, VNQ, XBI, XLE, XLK, XLP, XLY, XOP

Monthly Task

1. Calculate the performances of last month (about 20 trade days) of the ETFs in Portfolio 8 (i.e. GDX, IYF, IYH, KBE, KRE, OIH, RTH, SMH, UNG, USO, VNQ, XBI, XLE, XLK, XLP, XLY and XOP).
2. Replace the current ETF with the top-performed ETF if you have not owned it. If so, do nothing.

More hints

Keep track of your ETF performance of the two portfolios by obtaining the prices from one of many free sites such as Yahoo!Finance. It is easy to calculate the returns using a spreadsheet could speed up the process. Here is the formulae.

Return of last month =(Current Price - Last Month Price)/abs(Last month Price)
Return of 2 months = (Current Price - Price 2 months ago)/abs(Price 2 months ago)

"abs function" ensures correctness when both prices are negative.

The above is my suggestions. Feel free to include ETFs in the portfolios. Do paper trading until you're comfortable to use real money.

For diversification, do it bi-monthly (but still keep the ETFs for a month) or use all 2 strategies with 2 portfolios each, so you have more different ETFs. Recommend 5% from the current price for stop orders, so in theory, you lose about 5% max in every trade.

Improve your performance
- Watch out for the peak and the ETF could drop fast and vice versa for bottom. One metric is RSI(14). If it is over 70, it is likely overbought.
- Watch out for ETFs that have increased value by more than 5%. There are several trades with losses more than 10%.
- Check P/E of the ETF. If it is over 25, most likely it is over-priced. Get it from http://www.multpl.com/.
- For overbought and over-valued ETFs, set trailing stop (i.e. stops on the current price, not the initial buy price).
- Check its SMA-20% and SMA-50% from Finviz.com. They should be positive.
- Also, as described in this book, some sectors perform better in different stages of a market cycle.
- The second book (included) has many sector rotation ideas.

- Start with ETFs that are commission free from your broker and also check out the ETF's expenses.
- When you are ready to expand your testing, try ETFReplay. They do not pay me anything except let me use the subscription for a restricted period.

Why most ETF rotation strategies fail

1. Do not time the market. I include a simple method.
2. Strategies do not work in the current market. If the strategy fails, do not use it until it works again.
3. Not using stops especially on volatile ETFs such as biotech.
4. The ETF may be peaking and could fall very fast. Include metrics such as P/E, RSI(14) and huge change of SMA-20.

Section II: Market timing

The first chapter in this section tries to convince you how important market timing is. If it is too boring, skip the calculations or the entire chapter to continue to how to detect market plunges in the chapter titled Death Cross.

1   The power of market timing

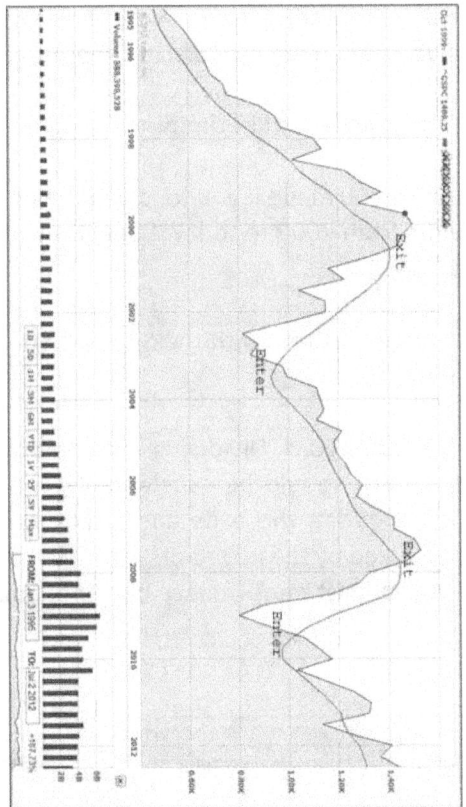

Most e-book readers allow you to select the graph to make it fit entirely on your screen. I use SPY, an ETF simulating the market. Detecting market plunges as seen in this graph indicates the exit points and reentry points also from 2000 to 9-2009 as follows.

Market Plunge	Peak	Bottom	Indicator Exit	Indicator Reenter
2000	08/28/00	09/20/02	10/01/00	06/01/03
2007	10/12/07	03/06/09	02/01/08	09/01/09
			08/01/11	11/01/11

Table: Vital Dates

For simplicity I skipped a few brief exits and reentries since 2011. You can run the simple chart once a month. When it indicates a potential market plunge is close, run the chart once a week. The last row represents a false signal.

This is based on stock prices so it may not identify the peaks and bottoms precisely, but so far it has not failed to avoid big losses and ensure big gains by reentering the market. I hope the next market plunge would give us enough time to act as these two did.

Unbelievable return with market timing

Calculate how much you made if you followed the above exit points and reenter points from 2000 to today. I bet you would have made a good fortune.

I compared the above returns with the SPY without market timing from 1-2000 to 9-2013.

There are many assumptions. Dividends and compounding are not considered. My return should be substantially better if I include buying contra ETFs during the exits and selling them during the reentries. I was shocked by the incredible return by using this simple market timing. Again, past performance does not guarantee future performances.

Summary info:

S&P 500 1-2000 to 9-2013	With Market Timing	Without Market Timing
Better	**500%**	
Gain	1,000	167
Gain %	68%	11%
Annualized gained	5%	1%
Days	4,959	4,959

Calculations:

S & P 500	With Market Timing	Without Market Timing
1-2000	1,469[1]	1,469[1]
Exit 10/01/00	1,041[2]	1,041
Enter 06/01/03	1,041	964[4]
Exit 02/01/08	1,489[3]	1,379[4]
Enter 09/01/09	1489	1,020[5]
Exit 08/01/11	1,888	1,293
Enter 11/01/11	1,888	1,251
09/03/13	2,469	1.638
Gained	2,469 – 1,469=1,000	1,638-1,469=167
Gain %	1000/1469 = 68%	167/1469 = 11%
Annualized gained	68% * 365/4959=5%	11%*365/4959=1%
Better	(1,000-167)/167 = 500%	

Portfolio with Market Timing:

[1] Both start with S&P 500 of 1,469 on 1-3-2000.
[2] 10/01/00
The market timing portfolio exits the market and remains the same value of 1,041 until 6/1/00.
[3]   02/01/08
The market timing portfolio exits the market and remains the same value of 1,489 until 9/1/09.

'1,489' is calculated as follows:
1,041 * (1 + Rate) = 1,041 * (1 + 1,379-964)/964) = 1,489
where the S&P 500 is 964 on 6/1/00 and 1,379 on 2/1/08.

The other calculations are based on the S&P 500 at 1,020 on 9/1/9, 1,293 on 8/1/11, 1,251 on 11/1/11 and 1,636 on 9/3/13.

Portfolio without Market Timing:

[1] Both starts with the S&P 500 of 1,469 on 1-3-2000. We could use the 9/3/13 the S&P 500 value, but it would not account for some compounded interest considerations.

[4] S&P 500 is 964 on 6/1/00 and 1,379 on 2/1/08.

[5] 02/01/08. The portfolio value is calculated to be 1,020 as follows:
1,379 * (1 + Rate) = 1,379 * (1 + (1020-1379)/1379) = 1,020
where S&P 500 is 1,379 on 2/1/08 and 1,020 on 9/1/09.

The other calculations are based on the S&P 500 at 1,293 on 8/1/11, 1,251 on 11/1/11 and 1,636 on 9/3/13.

I cannot believe the shocking return with market timing. I checked my calculations and there was nothing wrong that I could find.

2   Simplest market timing

Why market timing

Before 2000, market timing was a waste of time. However after that, we have had two market plunges with the average loss of about 45%. It sounds harder to time the market than it actually is. We have a simple technique to detect market plunges and when to reenter the market. Our objective is reducing the loss to 25%.

Market timing depends on charts; the following describes how to use chart information without creating charts. Most charts will not identify the peaks and bottoms of the market as they depend on data (i.e. the stock prices). However, it would reduce further loses. It is simpler than it sounds. Just follow the procedure below.

The first part of this technique detects market plunges, and the second part advises you when to reenter the market. It applies to individual stocks too.

How to detect market plunges without charts (a.k.a. <u>Death Cross</u>)

1. Bring up Finviz.com.

2. Enter SPY (or any ETF that simulates the market).

3. If SMA-200% is positive, it indicates that the market plunge has not been detected and you can skip the following steps.

4. The market is plunging if SMA-50% is more negative than SMA-200%. To illustrate this condition, SMA-200% is -2% and SMA-50% is -5%.

5. Sell most stocks starting with the riskiest ones first such as the ones with negative earnings, high P/Es and/or high Debt/Equity. Obtain this info from Finviz.com by entering the symbol of the stock you own.

6. Conservative investors should sell only those over-priced stocks. Aggressive investors should sell all stocks. Extremely aggressive investors should sell all stocks, buy contra ETFs, and even short stocks. I do not recommend beginners to be aggressive.

When to return to the market (a.k.a. Golden Cross)

Use the above in a reversed sense to detect whether the market has been recovering. However, when the SMA-200% turns positive, I would start buying value stocks (low P/E but the 'E' has to be positive, and/or low Debt/Equity).

1. Bring up Finviz.com.

2. Enter SPY (or any ETF that simulates the market).

3. If SMA-200% is negative, the market is not recovering, and you can skip the following steps.

4. Sell all contra ETFs and close all shorts if you have any.

5. Market recovery is confirmed when SMA-50% is more positive than SMA-200%. To illustrate this condition, SMA-200% is 2% and SMA-50% is 5%. Commit a large percent of cash (or all cash for aggressive investors) to stocks. If you do not know what to buy, buy SPY or an ETF that simulates the market.

Do the above once a month. When the SPY price is closer to SMA actions percentage, perform the above once a week. The charts and data for market timing described in this book are based on SMA-350 (Simple Moving Average) that is more preferable than this simple procedure, but it requires some simple charting.

3   Market timing by calendar

The following predictions are based on historical data. You may have slightly different findings depending on when you start and when you end your testing.

You can load the historical data of SPY via Yahoo!Finance and check out how close you are or different from my own predictions. They are my predictions based on historical data. Use it as a reference only.

- Presidential cycle.
  Usually the market performs worse in the first two years after the election than the next two. During the 3rd year the president has to make the economy look rosy in order to buy votes. Statistically it is the best year for the market and is followed by a good year (the election year). The government may stimulate the economy, the stock market and employment by printing more money, lowering interest rates and lowering taxes. The market in the 100 days before the election should be positive and less volatile according to 40 years of data.

  Democratic presidents have better market performance statistically than Republican presidents. This is not too logical as though Republicans are more pro-business traditionally.

- Olympics.
  It has been proven that the host country has a better chance that its stock market appreciates the year after the Olympics. It could be due to the exposure from the Olympics and / or the huge expenses in preparing for the Olympics.

  The last two Olympics follow this pattern as of 12/23/2013:

Olympics Country / Year	ETF	Period	Return
United Kingdom / 2012	EWU	Jan. 3, 2013 - Dec. 23,2013	11%
China / 2008	FXI	Jan. 3, 2009 - Dec. 31, 2009	43%

Greece could be an exception. It is too small a country to host this world-class event and it has wasted too many resources by building too many white elephants that the country can never justify. Brazil depends on its export of natural resources to China, so I do not count on the Olympics effect there.

Winning a lot of Olympic medals has no prediction for the stock markets. Both the Russian Empire and E. Germany were winners but disappeared in their original forms afterwards.

- Seasonal.
  Best profitable investment period is: Nov. 1 to April 30 of the following year. It is similar to the saying 'Sell in May and Go away'. It did not work since 2009 as it was an Early Recovery (defined by me) in the market cycle.

  The market does not always happen as predicted. However, when more folks follow this, it becomes a self-fulfilling prophecy. I prefer "Sell on April 15 and come back on Oct. 15" to act before the herd. The more practical strategy is to start selling in April 1 and become more aggressive (selling at closer to the market prices) when it is close to May 1. For the last five years, I did not find this prediction reliable.

  The explanation of the 'summer doldrums' could be that the investors cash their stocks for vacations and college tuition in the fall. Buying quality companies at the dips could be profitable.

- The worst month: September.
  The next worst month is October. However, if there is no serious market crash during October (and this month has more than its shares of crashes), it could be the best month to buy stocks.

- The best month for the bull: November.
  However, several market bottoms occurred in October and November. The next strong month is December.

- Best 30 days: Dec. 15 to Jan. 15, next year.
  It was correct for the period of 2012-2013.

- Window dressing.
  Institutional investors sell their losers and buy winners around Nov. 1. From my rough estimate and on the average, the winners have a 2% percentage point gain better than the market and the losers have 1% worse than the market.

I recommend that you evaluate the top 10 winners from the last 10 months or YTD in Oct. 15 and sell them at 3% gain or two months later.

I recommend that you buy in Dec. and sell them 3 months later. Include the stocks with more than 30% loss for the last 11 months or YTD, sort them by Earning Yield in descending order and evaluate the top 10 stocks.

In both cases, do not buy foreign stocks and stocks with return of capital. Ignore stocks not in the three major exchanges, with low volumes and stock prices less than $2. Do not buy in losing years such as 2007 and 2008. I have my tests with my own assumptions and I use tools not available to most readers.

This is a guideline only. Do not buy any stocks during market plunges. Current events should be considered first such as a potential war and the hiking of interest rates.

Afterthoughts

- I predict it will be a sideways market in the later part of 2013. I am following the sideways strategy: Buy on dips and sell when the market is ups. One's prediction.

- Why September has a bad reputation?
  http://www.marketwatch.com/story/betting-on-septembers-terrible-odds-2013-08-27?dist=beforebell

  The September of 2013 (2 days away at the time of this writing) will have more problems. Check it out how many of the following are correct on Oc. 1, 2013. Use it as a future guideline to predict the next September using the current market conditions then:

  1. The market is not excessively expensive, but it is not cheap. It is due for a 5% correction.
  2. Unrest in Syria (check any unrest in your next prediction on September).
  3. High oil prices due to Syria.
  4. September is statistically a bad month for the stock market. However, it could be an opportunity to invest after the correction if any.
  5. Interest rates is rising.

6. All the above indicate the market will dip. However, the rosier outlook is that the global economies are improving even slowly.

- January effect.
  The performance of January may determine how the entire year performs. I cannot find any rationale but it has been proven right statistically.

- Earnings period announced in Jan., April, July and Oct. would cause big swings in stocks when they have surprises. Earning revisions could be a good predictor.
  http://www.investopedia.com/terms/e/earningsseason.asp

Links
Presidential Cycle:
http://www.investopedia.com/articles/financial-theory/08/presidential-election-cycle.asp

Calendar-based market timing:
http://stock-chartist.com/2010/10/calendar-based-market-timing/

Calendar market timing for 2013:
http://www.investorecho.com/archives/8047

Filler: Golden Gate

Just minutes ago, my mail system asked me to sign in. I did and repeatedly they asked me to sign in again and again. I closed down everything and followed Gates' golden rule: If everything does not work, just power down everything and power it up again. I did this and prayed too. It works. Thanks Gates for fixing my problem.

There is NO one doing BASIC quality control. If it happened in my generation, many guys would be fired. Mediocrity is the new norm?

4   Market timing example

The market is making new highs. There are always two camps of market timers. One camp predicts a crash is coming while the other predicts it will continue making new highs. This article includes both arguments and suggests how and what actions you need to take to protect your investments.

Management summary

The market is fundamentally unsound evidenced by fundamental metrics but technically sound evidenced by technical metrics that both will be described in this article. The data were obtained on 09/22/2018. The market has not changed a lot as of 01/2020.

Suggested actions

No one predicts the market correctly and consistently. Otherwise there are no poor folks. Moving the risky investments such as most stocks to cash too early would miss the potential profits. Moving it too late would risk the loss of your stocks.

Your actions depend on your risk tolerance. If you are conservative such as a retiree, you may want to have a larger portion of your investments in lower risk such as CDs and bonds. You can take one of the following three actions or combine all of the three actions.

1. When the market turns to technically unsound, it is time to move your stocks to cash. The market timing indicators may give false signals. In this case, the indicator would tell you to move back to stocks. Most likely you do not lose much except dealing with the consequences of taxes in non-retirement accounts.
2. Move a portion of your risky investments into cash, laddered CDs and/or short-term bonds. Again, the size of the portion depends on your risk tolerance.
3. Use stops. The sell orders would be changed to market orders when the stocks dip below prices specified by you. I prefer to use SPY or other ETF to determine the market direction. Some sectors and some stocks move faster than others. In one crash, my energy stocks were still profitable while the market was tanking. Eventually these energy stocks caught up and fell fast. Today's highly profitable stocks are FAANG stocks as a group.

I propose and prefer 'manual stop orders' to prevent market manipulation. However, usually large ETFs cannot be manipulated easily. Manipulators try to profit from your stop orders. Set a stop order price in your `mind. When the stock falls to that specified price, sell it via a market order.

My friend confirmed my "manual stop order":

"High-frequency trading via Algo Trading Strategy can see exactly where pre-set trailing stops are and sweep across them (play them) like strings on a violin. Pre-set a trailing stop and it is bound to be triggered because Algo hunt them down. Then watch the market rip higher."

Analysis: Fundamentals and Technical

It consists of Fundamental Analysis and Technical Analysis. The former measures how expensive the current market is and the latter measures the trend of the market.

Many metrics were obtained from Finviz.com as of 9/22/2018 while others are obtained from other websites. With the exception of Fidelity.com, all websites described here are free and readily available. It also serves as a guide on how you can do your own market timing especially after a few months.

The following chart uses SPY to represent the market of the top 500 stocks. It is market cap weighted. It means the higher the market cap the stock, the higher percent of the stock is represented in the index. It turns out most are riskier FAANG stocks.

Enter Finviz.com in your browser and enter SPY. I am not responsible for any errors.

Indicator	Pass	Current Value	Indicating
• Technical			
Death Cross[1]		SMA-50 = 2.3% & SMA-200 = 6.3%	Pass
Technical Analysis: 350 SMA%[2]	>0	Price above the SMA-350.	Pass
RSI(14)	<70	61	Pass
Duration (yr.)	<5	10	Fail
		Overall	**Pass**
• Fundamental			
Valuation			
P/E[3]	<15.7	25.4	High by 62%. Fail.

Shiller P/E[3]	<16.6	33.5	High by 102%. Fail
P/B[3]	<2.78	3.52	High by 27%. Fail.
P/S[3]	<1.50	2.33	High by 55%. Fail.
Oil price	30-100	70.71	Pass
Interest rate[6] T-Bill 1 months[7]	<5	2.05	Pass
T-Bill 3 months[7]	Yield	2.18	
T-Bill 30 years[7]	Curve	3.20	Pass
Flow to Equity[4]		-3.371M	Fail
Flow to bond[4]		7.206M	
Corporate debt/GDP[8]	<40	45%	High by 13%. Fail.
USD[5]		Strong	Fail
Gold		High	Fail
Bubble		Several	Fail
Market experts		Fear long term	Neutral
Politics		Trump	Fail
Misc.		Trade war	Fail
		Overall	**Fail**

[1] This is the market timing technique without using a chart.

[2] I tried to use SMA-400% to reduce false signals without success.

[3] Get it from http://www.multpl.com/ Same as CAPE.

[4] Get it from https://www.ici.org/research/stats. It is based on 09-12-18. "Flow to Equity" is based on domestic ETF estimate. Treat it as two phases in moving to equity. First phase of moving excessively to equity indicates the market is peaking. The second phase indicates the market is plunging when flow of equity is excessively negative.

[5] Global corporations will suffer in profits converted back to USD and hard to sell to foreign countries. [4] Get it from the above link.

[6] Rising interest is bad for corporations and high-ticket products, but good for lenders.

[7] Get it from https://www.treasury.gov/resource-center/data-chart-center/interest-rates/Pages/TextView.aspx?data=yield based on 09/21/18

[8] With the low interest rate, it may not be that critical. Corporations take advantage of the low interest rate.

Overall

Overall, technical is fine as the market is making new highs. Many aggressive investors exit the market on technical indicators only as the over-valued market could linger on for a long term such as from 2009 to 2017 so far.

Overall, fundamental is not sound. The increasing market price also is decreasing the fundamental metrics such as P/E, P/B and P/S. It is bad unless there is reason to support such as the fast earnings growth in 2009.

Many metrics are deteriorating

RSI(14) is getting closer to 65 (a passing grade specified by me).

Inverse yield curve (1.5 vs. 2.33) is about 61% apart from my interpretation and calculation. It is not a warning now but we should keep an eye on it. Most market crashes have occurred when it is 0% or negative. The theory is that in a normal case the short-term interest rates should be lower than the long-term interest rate.

Another source calculates it is 1.1% and that is very close to inversion since the last recession. From MarketWatch, the 30-year fixed interest rates is 4.66% and 1-year rate is 3.96% giving an inverse yield curve 18% apart, which is quite alarming.

Mathematically incorrect, today's full employment is at 4%. Most recessions are closely preceded by troughs in unemployment and the reverse for economy recovery.

GDP growth has been predicted from 1.8% to 3%. The 3% is from the White House for their obvious purpose. I predict it will pop up due to meeting the tariff deadlines, tax cuts and spending increases. It will then be declining to 2%. A healthy US economy should maintain 3% without special factors such as excessive immigration.

We have record debts: investors' margin, corporate debt and Federal debt. These are bubbles going to burst. Federal debt / GDP is about 95% (https://fred.stlouisfed.org/series/gfdegdq188S) today. It does not predict the market performance as this ratio was 53% and 55% before the last two market crashes. It will affect the long-term performance of the economy when we have to service the huge national debt.

We do have 10 years of stock growth at the expense of record Federal deficit. Thanks to President Obama from investors and no thanks from next generations who have to pay back our national debt. It is overdue for a correction. Hopefully it is not a crash which has an average loss of about 45%. We did have two recent corrections losing more than 10%: 2011-12 EU debt crisis and 2014-16 oil crash. The oil price has been rising from $30 per barrel to today's $70. It is still a long way from my warning of $120.

Potential triggers
Trade wars with China, Canada or EU will be the strongest trigger. Our most profitable companies are virtually all international companies. They need fair trade to prosper.

The other trigger is the possible impeachment of President Trump.

Check the validity of our charts
It seems some metrics vary. It could use after hour trading. It could be the "Days" may be "Sessions" – calendar day is different from trading session. I selected 10 years for most of the charts and StockCharts let me select only 5 years.

Here is a list of sites for charts.
https://www.stocktrader.com/2013/12/10/best-free-stock-chart-websites/
These are the three sites I use a lot: Fidelity (customers only), StockCharts and Finviz.com (missing some metrics).

As stated before, SPY may not be the best to represent the market. I prefer an ETF for 1,000 stocks and weigh the stocks evenly (i.e. not according to the market cap). Google "market timing 2020 (or current year)" for more expert info. Here is one.

Mid-year update

Basically nothing significant has changed recently: The market is fundamentally unsound and technically sound after the recent rally. The only update is our national debt is skyrocketing. Today's "Debt/GDP" is similar to the market height in 2000 and we know what happened afterwards. That's why Buffett has accumulated a lot of cash now.

Even with the unlimited QE (i.e. printing money excessively), the high inflation and market crash predicted by many experts have not been materialized so far. This is my third prediction in "Disaster of 2020". The status of USD as a reserve currency will be shaken; I do not know when, as I do not have a time machine.

Why the market keeps going up while the economy is going down? The Fed has provided a lot of cash and the cash is chasing a fixed number of assets such as gold and stocks. It is the simple, proven theory of demand and supply. It will continue for a while as long as there is unlimited supply of money. At some point, it will pop. At that time, it could lead to a long recession, unless the economy improves as it did in 2009. The smart Fed chairman knows how it will harm the country by excessively printing money. However, he has to obey his boss who is seeking for reelection.

I expect we are in a prolonged period of low interest rates and even negative interest rates. When the rates are negative, our Treasury bonds are no longer marketable. The foreign central banks including China would dump our national debts if it has not been already started. The economy is dressed up nicely in an election year. Giving us free money is the easy way to buy votes, but the long-term effects are very harmful.

Using cheap money to buy back the company's stock would boost the stock price and hence make the management wealthier. It is a false sense of the stock value. When the company cannot pay back the debt obligations, the company would go bankrupted. If the U.S. were a company, she has gone bankrupted already.

As of 6/15/2020, QQQ (representing NASDAQ stocks) has been up 11% YTD and it is far better than DIA (representing DOW stocks) and SPY (representing the 500 large stocks in the S&P Index and losing about 5% YTD). QQQ has a lot of tech stocks while DIA has a lot of losers including Boeing. Most FAANG stocks are making record highs and QQQ is market cap weighed.

Most of the ETFs on chips have been up more than 40% in a year. I bought Amazon and two chip ETFs. I use trailing stops to protect my portfolio. Huawei is buying a lot of U.S. chips in the 120-day relaxed period. In September this year and if there is no extension, I would sell these chip ETFs fast.

I have used the strategy described in my book "Profit from the recovery of the pandemic" to take advantage of this volatile market. I used 5% as the threshold and I had too few trades; now I changed to 3%. Expecting a market crash, I weigh more on contra ETFs. As described in the same book, I bought a lot of contra ETFs, GLD and the stock of a gold miner. It is for insurance. ETFs on oil is my big mistake.

If the U.S.D. loses the status of reserve currency (not likely soon), it would bring prolonged depression and high inflation in the U.S. In this case, it is safer to invest in real estate, precious metals and profitable companies than in CDs and bonds that would lose values due to inflation.

Check out many articles on the status of the current market. Many have opposing views, so you have to make your own decision. In any case, play it safe with stops. Here is one article from MarketWatch.com.

Canary warning?

When I was working on my new book "Best stocks to buy for 2021" on Dec. 10, 2020, I found something really strange. I have never rejected so many stocks that have Fidelity's Equity Summary Score higher than 9. I rejected them as there were a lot of dumping from the insiders. Insiders know their companies better than most of us. Is it the canary telling us the market is over-valued?

Initially the following stocks have been screened by my value screens. Buy any one of the following stocks, **only** if you have good reason(s).

Symbol	Fidelity Score	Insider Purchase
BCC	9.9	-24%
GPI	10.0	-17%
HEAR	10.0	-75%
HIBB	9.4	-30%
HVT	9.5	-37%
HZO	9.5	-27%

How can HEAR score a perfect 10 while the Insiders' Transaction is -75% (I treated -2% is normal). The analysts must be wrong this time, or they believe the market will continuously make new heights. Will update the performance results later to see who is wrong.

A correction or a crash?

In Dec., 2018, the S&P500 is about 15% down and a crash is about 45% down.

If a crash is coming, there should be additional 30% down. If it is a correction (15% average), then we have it already. Should we pick up bargains now? Or, are they bargains? It is a trillion dollar question.

We need a trigger for a market crash like the financial crisis in 2008 and the internet bubble in 2000. Besides the record-high margin debt, the possibility of Trump's impeachment and a trade war, I do not see any.

Filler: CIA mistook it as a missile silo in China.

5   Market cycle

"Bull markets are born on pessimism, grow on skepticism, mature on optimism, and die on euphoria" - Sir John Templeton

The stock market has cycles as our practical interpretation of the above. It is about five years apart, but it fluctuates widely. I divide it into four stages: Bottom, Early Recovery, Up and Peak.

My defined four stages of a market cycle

We need to apply the right investing strategies to each of the four stages of the cycle.

- **Bottom**

    I would not invest for at least the first six months (or even a year) after the big plunge starts, which could lose over 25% in a few months time. The exceptions are investing in contra ETFs and selling short for aggressive investors.

    I estimate it will take a year from the start of the plunge to the bottom, so I will normally sell stocks early in the plunge and do not buy stocks that are in the sector (sometimes sectors) that causes the bubble for about two years after the plunge.

    At the bottom, the high-yield corporate bonds (i.e. junk bonds) would prosper when the interest rates is decreasing to stimulate the economy.

    From mid-2007 to mid-2008, bonds suffered as the investors thought the sky was falling down - it was to those who lost the jobs and/or their houses. After that, some bonds especially the long-term bonds appreciated about 50% for the following year.

    The government lowered the interest rates and these bond prices with high interest rates surged. Correct timing in buying bonds could be very profitable.

    Long-term bonds have more impact by the interest rate: The lower the interest rate, the higher the bond prices of higher-yield bonds. The older bonds with higher interest rates are more valuable to the newer bonds with lower interest rates.

I define this period of the bottom from the start of the plunge to the start of Early Recovery.

- **Early Recovery**

It usually starts after one year from the plunge; no one can pin point the exact time consistently. By this time preferably earlier, we should have closed out all positions in contra ETFs and shorts.

Roughly speaking, October, 2007 (some use 2008) is the start of the market plunge. March, 2009 is the end of the bottom stage and the start of the early recovery stage of the 2007 cycle. However, every market cycle is different in where it starts and ends.

The one-year gain from the bottom is most profitable. It usually gains over 25% in a year from the market bottom. I, a conservative investor, had huge gains using some leverage in my largest taxable account in 2009. From my memory, I had a similar return in 2003 but I had not saved the statement as in 2009.

In this phase, value is a better parameter than growth in searching for stocks. If your investment subscription provides a composite value score and a composite timing score, the sort parameter of your screened stocks could be "Composite Value / Composite Timing" in descending order. Select the top stocks in this order. You still have to analyze the top-screened stocks.

Forward (same as Expected) P/E is a good metric. However, most companies may be losing money at this stage. Those companies that can last for more than one year with its cash reserve are potential good buys. The best appreciated stocks are beaten companies that have precious technologies and good customer bases. They could be candidates to be acquired if they are small enough.

- **Up**

Usually the growth metrics such as PEG could be better than the value metrics such as expected P/E during this phase. Most stocks are winners except contra ETFs and shorting stocks. When the growth stocks are making headlines and the defensive stocks are being dumped, this is the hint that we're well into the Up phase of the market cycle.

Locate stocks with growth metrics such as favorable PEG and high SMA-200% (from Finviz.com). Do not be scared on how much they have already appreciated. The strategy "Buy High and Sell Higher" works in this phase. Protect your profits with stops.

Ensure that they have value too. Skip the stocks with expected P/Es higher than 35 unless there are good reasons. Most stocks will gain due to the tide of the market. However, when they're overbought (RSI(14) over 60), be careful. When institutional investors sell these stocks, they will crash.

- **Peak**
  When everyone makes easy money and the interest rates is high, watch out. Stop loss and/or stop limit should be used to protect your investment. Check out whether there is any bubble that would be burst like the internet in 2000 and the finance (and housing) in 2007.

  Internet crisis is easy to spot, but not the financial crisis. In 2007 we had a cycle longer than the average which is about 5 years. The plunge is very fast and very steep – thanks to the institutional investors who drive the market down.

  Run the technical analysis chart described in the Chapter on Spotting Big Market Plunges at least monthly (weekly if you have time). Protect your investment. Do not fall in love with any stock (you can buy it back later at a deep discount). Making the last buck is a fool's game.

  Accumulate cash according to your risk tolerance. A retiree or a conservative investor would accumulate from 25% to 50% and should be ready to move to all cash when the plunge starts.

  We can lower the cash percent if we use enough stop loss protection. Be psychologically prepared because the stock market may still rise for a while. There is no perfect market timing.

The 2007 Cycle

The market plunged starting in 10-2007 and ending in 3-2009 (bottom), started to recover in 3-2009 (early recover), and trended up from 2010 to 1-2013 (the up phase of the market cycle). As of 3/2016, it is the peak phase defined by me.

As of 1/2013, we have recovered all the market losses since 2007. However, as of 7/2014, the economy has not fully recovered compared to the economy before the plunge. The employment judging by the medium salary has not fully recovered and the economy is not expanding. It is uncommon that the economy does not follow the market. It is due to the excessive supply of money by the government and partly due to globalization to allow companies to hire overseas.

Although a W-shaped recession seldom happens, we have a chance today. We hope we do not have a depression and/or the similar lost decades that Japan has been experiencing. Some may conclude we are close to completing a market cycle from 2007 to 2016. As of 2016, the economy is recovering slowly and we're better than most other global economies.

Again, market timing is not an exact science as it involves irrational human beings and government interventions. The timing using market cycle described here is a guideline as it is hard to time it exactly.

The average market cycle is about 5 years, but they fluctuate. If we consider 2007 as the plunge, we have about 8 years of this cycle as of 2015.

In a typical cycle (few are typical), we have about one year in each of the 4 phases I defined (plunge, early recovery, up and peak).

Events/Triggers

There are financial events and triggers that cause the transition of one phase of the market cycle to another. They usually do not change the sequence of the phases (say not from Peak to Early Recovery), but they may change the duration of the phase. Examples are:

- The government announcing change of the interest rate,

- Change of employment, and
- Change of GNP.

Sectors in a market cycle (my suggestion)

Market Phase	Favorable		Unfavorable
Early Recovery	Financial, Technology, Industrial		Energy, Telecom, Utilities
Up	Technology, Industrial, Housing		
Peak	Mineral, Health Care, Energy, Long-Term Bond, Consumer Discretionary		
Bottom	Consumer Staples, Utilities		Consumer Discretionary, Technology, Industrial, Long-Term & high-yield Bond

The sectors that cause the recession usually take a longer time to recover. In 2000, the technology sector was not favorable in the Early Recovery phase, contrary to the above table. In 2007, the financial sector was not favorable in the Early Recovery phase. These are the "offending" sectors that cause the plunges.

In a recession, we usually cannot cut down on consumer staples and utilities, but we can cut down on buying consumer gadgets. Companies usually postpone investing in equipment and systems during a recession and expand when the economy is humming. The government usually lowers the interest rates right after the plunge to stimulate the economy.

Conclusion

When the market is about to plunge or change from one stage to another, run the described chart more frequently and read more articles written by the experts.

Again, market timing is not an exact science but it is based on educated guesses. The better guesses should have more rights than wrongs in the long term. Our actions depend on our risk tolerance. Be careful on using any new strategy that has not been fully understood and proven. Since 2000, market timing is very important to your financial health with two market plunges with an average of about 45% loss.

6   Early recovery, best time for profit

I have 80% return in 2009 in my largest taxable account. I did not include it in my other books before as I just found out the written statement.

This is the best time to make a profit: Early Recovery defined in my stages of a market cycle (described next in Death Cross). My chart told me to start move to equity in September, 2009. I did in March, 2009 with other reasons. It could be luck, technique or both.

I did dip into my credit line of my equity loan (not recommended to most). I did not use it as a margin loan as most folks do, but as a saving from the lower rates than my broker's rate. I paid back the loan right after I sold some stocks. The turnaround was high until I exhausted my short-term losses (tax loss harvest).

The strategy is bottom fishing: finding value stocks. Some sectors described in my book are better in this stage of the market cycle.

I had similar success in 2003. I did not have defined bottom fishing technique at that time. I expected the market to be fully recovered in two years. From Value Line, I selected stocks with high Projected 3-5 year returns and the short-term assets can last for two years (judged by the burnt rates).

My experiences

I did not have the hints specified in my books until 2008.

- 2000 Exit. Moved most of my sector funds (most in tech) to traditional sectors after reading articles on how over-priced the internet stocks were. It would be more profitable if I moved them to cash. They did not have contra ETFs then. I could not short in my retirement accounts and I did not have experience in options.

- 2003 Return. I betted the market would return in two years. I bought many stocks which could survive in two years with the cash they had. I was lucky that the market returned in the same year. One stock was acquired by IBM with a huge gain.

- 2008 Exit. I did have the chart but I did not follow it. My big wins in energy stocks in 2007 gave me false security. When the market crashed, the energy stocks crashed too. I sold some stocks during the crash. I should have bought contra ETFs.

- 2009 Return. My chart told me to return in mid-March, 2009. I started buying in Feb., 2009. With the accumulated short-term capital losses, I traded stocks. I used my home equity loan that has far lower interest rates for my margin account. I used the margin account only to fill up the gaps between trades. Most of the time, the margin and the loan were zero. It could be my best year making about 80% profit in my largest taxable account.

Filler: Happy Mother's Day Poem

The following is my translation from poet Yu's work in Chinese. I changed some words as some could not be translated effectively. I added the title "Two Cries".

-------- Two Cries -----------

I cried at two unforgettable times in my life.

The first time when I came to this world.
The second time when you left this world.

The first time I did not know but from your mouth.
The second time you did not know but from my heart.

Between these two crises, we had endless laughs.
For the last 30 years, we had joyful laughs that had been repeated, repeated...

You treasured every laugh.
I cherish every laugh for the rest of my life.

Section III: Bonus

1   Sectors to be cautious with

There are many reasons to be very cautious when investing in the following sectors. However, Technical Analysis (a.k.a. charting) would give you more hints than the fundamentals for stocks in these sectors.

Loan companies/banks

The financial statements do not show the quality of their loan portfolios. Following this advice, you may be able to skip the banks that melted down in 2007. The peak of Citigroup is $550 and several banks   went   bankrupt.

Drug (generic is ok)

Understanding the complexities of the drug pipelines, its potential profits for new drugs and the expiration of its current drugs may not be worth the effort for most retail investors. In addition, a serious lawsuit and / or a serious problem with a drug could wipe out a good percentage of the stock price. When a drug shows unpromising sign(s) in any trial phase, the stock could plunge and vice versa.

Miners

It is extremely difficult to estimate how much ore (sometimes a miner owns several different types of ores and/or of different grades in the same or different mines) that the company has. It is further complicated by the complexities to extract and transport them. When the total of these costs is greater than its production price, the company will not be profitable. Understanding the market for ore futures is another discipline.

Many mining companies are in foreign countries such as Canada, Australia and countries in South America. Their financial statements of Canada and Australia are more trustworthy than those from most other emerging countries.

One potential problem of mining companies from many emerging countries is nationalization.

Mining rare earth ore is extremely risky when the profit depends on how China, a major producer of these ores, will price its ores. After China announced the export restrictions on rare earth elements, several non-Chinese companies announced to reopen their mines for rare earths but few have made any profits as of 2013. Developed countries have stricter environmental regulations.

Coal suffers from the rising use of cleaner oil and gas.

Insurance companies

Insurance companies profit by:

1. The difference between the total premiums received and the total claims minus expenses in running the company.

2. How well they invest your premiums; you pay your premiums earlier than you may collect from the claims.

They can protect the profits in #1 by restricting claims by natural disasters such as earthquakes and by re-insuring. However, a bad disaster could wipe out a lot of their profits.

Even if the insurance company shows you its investment portfolio, most of us, the retail investors, do not have the time and expertise to analyze it.

Emerging countries (not a sector)
Their financial statements especially from small companies cannot be trusted and many countries use different accounting standards. Emerging countries are where the economic growth is. I trade FXI, an ETF, rather than individual Chinese companies. I have lost a lot in small Chinese companies due to fraud. To check out whether the stock is an ADR, try ADR.COM.
https://www.adr.com/

Stocks with low volumes (not a sector)
Most likely you pay a high spread to trade these stocks. They can be manipulated easier. I remember when I had a hard time trying to sell

a stock of this kind. The majority of this company is owned by one person.

For simplicity, I trade stocks with the average daily trade volume over 6,000 shares (double it if the price is $2 or less). A better way could be in calculating the percent of your trade quantity / average daily trade volume to reduce the effect of penny stocks that have larger volumes due to the low prices. You need special skills to trade these stocks but it could be very profitable.

Good business and bad business

Banking is a good business. My deposit in them makes virtually zero interest, and they loan the same money making 3%. If they are more selective in loaning my money, they should make a good profit.

Restaurant is an easy business to open/run, but it is very hard to make good money. With the rising of minimal wages, it will get even tougher. That could be the reason for so many coupons today. The high-end restaurants are doing better due to the rising stock market. As of 8/2014, the new comers Noodles & Company (NDLS) and Potbelly (PBPB) are not doing very well.

Retailing is a tough business. Look at the top 10 retailers 15 years ago, I can only find two including Macy's that are still surviving. Most are either bankrupt or being acquired. Even Macy's was at one time in financial trouble and was rescued by the late Run Run Shaw in Hong Kong.
(http://tonyp4idea.blogspot.com/2014/08/on-retail.html)

#Filler: We're victims of our own success

A higher living standard means higher wages, more protections for our workers and more regulations for our environment. All these will make us less competitive.

2   Tax avoidance

Tax avoidance is a good way to save some money legally. Tax laws change all the time. Check Wikipedia on current investment taxes. Consult your tax lawyer as my knowledge in taxes is limited, and the tax laws are always changing.

In general for Federal returns on your taxable accounts (as opposed to IRA, Roth IRA, IRA-Rollover and 401K), you have to pay taxes on dividends either at the ordinary income rate or at a qualified rate which is usually lower. If the stock that was held longer than a year, you pay long-term capital tax (max. 20%). The short-term capital tax rate at the ordinary income rate up to 37%. In addition, you may have to pay state and local taxes. Currently, you can offset $3,000 or up to your total losses from your regular income.

Do not implement what I did as tax laws change frequently and every one's situation is different. Here is what I did and I hope it will be applicable to you.

- Sold most profitable stocks that I held more than a year in taxable accounts in 2011 to qualify for long-term capital gains. Usually they have more favorable tax treatments than the short-term capital gains, which are treated as ordinary income. I bought some back. I maintained a 15% tax bracket, so the tax bill from Uncle Sam is virtually 0 (not exactly due to more tax on social security and Medicare as a result of the trades). I still had to pay state tax. As a retiree, I can control my income.

- Converted part of my Rollover IRA to Roth in 2012 and 2013. I paid taxes today. However, the Roth conversion gives me tax-free appreciation for the future trades in this account and it will lower taxes and my minimum withdrawal requirement in the future. Check whether it is still available.

- The taxes from dividends in the retirement accounts are deferred but eventually they will be treated as regular income when they are withdrawn. Very few people have higher income during their retirement. If you are the lucky few due to the successful investing in your retirement accounts, you may end up with a higher tax bracket during your retirement, particularly when you are forced to withdraw at age 70 ½.

- Gifted some appreciated stocks to my children. The current price of the gifted stock is used in calculating the total cost allowed, not the price you paid for them. I prefer the value stocks that have potential for long-term appreciation. It is good for them and not good for Uncle Sam. You can gift up to $15,000 (in 2019) for each spouse to each child without paying any Federal tax. For a family of four, you and your spouse can gift up to $60,000 (= 15,000 * 4) a year.

  The link: https://www.irs.gov/businesses/small-businesses-self-employed/frequently-asked-questions-on-gift-taxes

  The cost basis of the transferred stock is quite complicated. Check out the current tax law. The cost basis of the appreciated stocks are carried to the receiver, so it would lower your capital taxes as most of us are in higher tax brackets than our children.

  From my experience, the cost basis of the depreciated stocks after the transfer is the market price on the transfer day as of 2016. I do not understand it enough to comment but just to tell you what I have experienced. I tried to offset my son's unexpected short-term capital gain by transferring a losing stock and that does not work.

- My lawyer set up trusts for me including my house. They will avoid probate hopefully. From the current tax law (as of 2016), the cost basis of your stocks will be stepped up or down to the stock prices on that day you pass away. Ask your heirs to keep a business paper for the stock prices or tell your brokers to adjust the cost basis on the day you pass away. Of course, you have to tell your heirs now to take care of these tasks. Again, ask your tax lawyer for details.

  Make sure you specify the beneficiaries in your and your spouse's accounts to avoid probate. Check your local state laws. Some states take more than a year to finish the probate process for a house. As of 2014, my state (Mass.) has an exemption of 1 million, not portable to your spouse, and they calculate the entire estate when it exceeds the exemption. There is no estate tax if my estate is a million dollar. I have to pay a rate on 1,000,001 if it just exceeds it by one dollar. That's why we should move 30 miles north to New Hampshire.

I estimate that it takes about three years for the average estate to be distributed. You want to cut down the duration by having a will to start with, so you do not want to pay extra for your lawyer.

- At age 70 ½ (as of 2016), you are required to withdraw them in a schedule and it could put you in higher tax bracket. Roth withdrawal is not counted in the mandatory withdrawal for a person's lifetime as of 2016.

- Roth IRA if qualified could be the best deal for most. However, you have to use after-tax money to fund your Roth IRA.

- I simulate my next year via my tax preparation software and adjust my income accordingly.

- Most oil partnerships and many MLPs require you to file special tax forms for non-retirement accounts in 2017. I avoided most of them as my time is limited. Some ETFs require you to file the complicated K-1 (vs 1099) in your tax return. You can find this requirement in ETFdb.com. You can avoid them by not buying these ETFs; I prefer to buy them in my non-taxable accounts (i.e. retirement accounts). Usually the taxes on these dividends are lowered as they are treated the return of investment after depreciation.

- Avoid wash sales in your taxable accounts
  http://en.wikipedia.org/wiki/Wash_sale

  You cannot claim the loss for the year if you buy back the stock within 30 days. Before I buy, I check whether I sold this loser in the last 30 days. Before I sell a loser, I check whether I bought it in the last 30 days.

  I placed one order to sell a loser at a higher price and another one to buy it back at a lower price. When there is a big swing in price for that stock, both orders were executed within 30 days. I cannot claim the loss of the sold stock for that year. However, the loss can be adjusted to the cost basis of the newly-acquired stock as of 2013.

There are many ways to avoid it. Try not to buy it back within 30 days (check the current regulation) and this is the best way. IRS has more restrictions and it is better not to push it to the limit. Buy a similar stock in the same sector. Buy it in your children's account. Again, check the current tax laws.

Afterthoughts

- Tax audit signs.
  http://money.cnn.com/gallery/pf/taxes/2014/03/14/tax-audit/index.html?iid=HP_LN
  Your business would be treated as a hobby if you do not have a profit in three out of the last five years. Day traders and businesses can deduct all the trading expenses. Some form an investing company in some Caribbean island to avoid paying taxes. Again check the current tax laws.

- As of 2013, the dividend tax is at 20% max. Do not believe it is no tax in tax-deferred accounts. When you withdraw, it will be treated as a regular income and it can be as high as almost 40% (as of 2013). Your dividend tax rate depends on your income.

- When you trade 5 times or more a week, investigate whether you're eligible to trade as a business by the current tax rule. A business allows its owner to deduct business expenses.

- Fidelity: Investment tax.
  https://www.fidelity.com/learning-center/mutual-funds/tax-implications-bond-funds
  ETF Taxes on Foreign Stocks:
  http://seekingalpha.com/article/2491465-foreign-withholding-taxes-in-international-equity-etfs

Links

Tax Avoidance:
http://en.wikipedia.org/wiki/Tax_avoidance
Tax Law:
http://en.wikipedia.org/wiki/Income_tax_%28U.S.%29
Without paying (gift tax):
http://en.wikipedia.org/wiki/Gift_tax_in_the_United_States#Gift_tax_exemptions
http://www.irs.gov/Businesses/Small-Businesses-&-Self-Employed/What%27s-New---Estate-and-Gift-Tax
AMT: http://en.wikipedia.org/wiki/Alternative_minimum_tax
Estate planning fun.
http://tonyp4idea.blogspot.com/2014/08/estate-planning-101-for-me.html

3   Technical analysis (TA)

The basics

Technical analysis (a.k.a. charting) is easier to learn than you might expect. It represents the trend of the market (a stock or a group of stocks) graphically. If more investors are in the market, the market would move upwards until it changes direction. We divide the trends into short-term, intermediate-term and long-term.

The chartists usually do not consider fundamentals as they believe they have already been priced into the stock price and some fundamentals are not available to the public. To illustrate, a new drug has been discovered, the stock price of the company jumps initially by insiders purchases and the informed. Its fundamental metrics do not demonstrate this right away, but many investors are buying to boost up the stock price as evidenced by the technical indicators such as SMA for 20 or 50 days.

The volume is a confirmation. When the stock moves up or down by 10% with a low volume, the trend is not yet confirmed.

The trend of the stock price is not a straight line in most cases. Hence a trend line is usually drawn to indicate the direction of the stock. Many investors believe the stocks fluctuate in certain ranges (i.e. channels) and the chart draws the upper value (the resistance line) and the lower value (the support line). In theory, the price of a stock fluctuates within the resistance line (ceiling for understanding) and support (floor). When it reaches its support, it becomes a buy and vice versa for a sell. Most charts including Finviz.com would display these lines.

When the price passes out of the channel, it is called a breakout. Darvas, one of the oldest and most successful chartists, profited from the breakouts of the resistance line and believed the stock was close to the support line of the new channel. Hence it would be a long way up in theory.

If it were so simple, there will be no poor folks

It works most of the time, but do not place all your money on it. For chartists, 51% is great (the same for playing Black Jack). Some trends reverse very fast such as the bio drug stocks in 2015. You need to hedge your bets such as placing stop orders. Most do not want to spend their lives in watching the trend from a big screen.

Most novices use too many technical indicators and lose in their performances to the professionals. Recently, most chartists were not doing all that great and I did not find many books on their success than a decade ago. It could be due to too many followers in similar setups. I verified it with my recent testing using Finviz.com.

Simple Moving Average

The basic technical indicator is SMA-N. It is the average of the last N trade sessions. When N is 20 (or SMA-20), we classify it as short-term. Similarly, SMA-50 is an intermediate-term and SMA-200 is long-term. I prefer 50, 100 and 250. This trend duration is important. For example, do not want to place long-term purchases using the short-term SMA-50. There are many modifications to SMA such as giving more weight to recent data, but I have not found them any better. Finviz.com includes this information without charting (SMA-20, SMA-50 and SMA-100 in percentages).

Defining the trend periods is rather arbitrary. I use SMA-350 to detect the market plunges and SMA-100 for stocks. Weighted Moving Average weighs more weight on recent price data.

It can be used to determine whether we are in bull, bear or a sideways market using SMA-50 (or SMA-200 for longer term) for the market (using SPY), the sector (using an ETF for the sector and the specific stock. The trend is up when it the price is above the SMA and the reversal of the trend.

https://www.youtube.com/watch?v=jdYNaE5GJ0k&list=WL&index=5&t=609s

The trend is your best friend
Most traders use TA for trending in a short duration. Investors can also use TA to time the entry and exit points for better potential profits. Value investors usually are patient and they do bottom

fishing and they search for 'oversold' condition using RSI(14). Again high volume is a confirmation.

Many sites provide charting free of charge such as Yahoo!Finance. Finviz.com provides a lot of technical indicators without charting such as SMA% and RSI(14). It also provides screen searching for stocks that meet your technical analysis criteria.

Hands on

Bring up Finviz.com and enter any stock symbol such as AAPL. You can see the daily prices of AAPL from about nine months ago to today. Three SMAs (Simple Moving Average) are displayed as SMA-20, SMA-50 and SMA-200. The first two are for short-term trends. When the price is above the SMA, it is expected to be trending up. Again, the trade volume is used as a confirmation.

You can also see the resistance line and the support line drawn. In theory, the stock will trade within these lines. When it exceeds its resistance line, it is called a breakout, and vice versa for a breakdown. Sometimes it displays some technical patterns such as Cup and Shoulder and Double Down (both are positive patterns).

Select Weekly data. The Candle chart is better described than the Daily chart. Candles give us better descriptions of the price: open, close, high and low. The green color indicates the price is up for the period (a week in this example) and the red color indicates a down period.

In addition, Finviz.com includes some technical indicators in the metric section such as RSI. Most other chart sites are similar in the basics. Use Finviz's Help and select Technical Analysis for more description. Investopedia has enhanced descriptions on this topic.

TA patterns

There are many TA patterns such as Bollinger Bands and MACD. The patterns are based on the stock prices and many times they prove to be correct predictions especially on stocks with high volume and high market caps. Patterns have been repeating themselves many times as they are driven by investors.

Sites for TA

There are many free sites for charts with explanations of their technical indicators. Popular ones include BigCharts.com, SmallCharts.com and Yahoo!Finance. Fidelity includes some unique features in its charts such as P/E.

Why I do not use TA as a primary tool for stock picking

My investing style is different from a day trader's. I prefer to 'Buy Low and Sell High' instead of 'Buy High and Sell Higher'. I try to find the real bottom price. TA will not find the bottom very easily but it tracks the trend better. As a bargain hunter, I do not expect the stock will rise fast as I'm usually swimming against the tide. However, value stocks could stay in the low price for a long time (i.e. value trap). I like to select stocks that turn around as evidenced by the SMA-20 and SMA-50.

With that said, my momentum portfolio has appreciated consistently and usually has the best performing stocks among all my portfolios. It is based on the timely grade from my subscriptions plus the metrics on timing.

Most chartists would also tell you to buy the stocks that have broken out (i.e. higher than the resistance line) and/or stocks at their highs. Contrary to value investing, you should exit when the trend reverses. The reversal could happen very fast and hence protect your portfolio by setting up stop loss (preferably with trailing stop) orders.

My opinion

I do not want to argue whether TA is good for you or not. You need to find that out. Most likely, the day traders and very short-term traders will profit more from TA than the investors seeking value stocks for the long-term gains.

Random remarks

Even if you do not use technical analysis, you should spend some time in learning it. It is better to marry fundamentals and TA. My random remarks are:

- The Institutional investors (insurance companies, pension funds, mutual funds, etc.) use TA and they MOVE the market. A lot of times it becomes a self-fulfilling prophecy. It is better to join them as most of us cannot beat them.

- Day traders take advantage of the institutional investors by spotting their trends.

- Most TA stocks should be good sized and have large average daily volumes. I prefer to use TA on value stocks to prevent long-term losses.

- I do know some folks making big money using TA, but I know more making good money using fundamentals. Since TA predicts the market better in the shorter term, its practitioners may have to pay higher taxes (in today's tax laws) in taxable accounts.

- Our objective should be making money with the least risk. Once you claim to belong to a certain group of either Fundamental or TA, you will be biased and forget your primary objective in investing.

- TA tracks the last two big market plunges (2000 and 2007) pretty well. The chart will not warn you right away for the upcoming plunge (as it depends on past data) to avoid the initial losses, but they will warn you to avoid bigger losses.

Afterthoughts

- Besides searching for stocks that have potential breakouts, we should check the stocks we owned for potential breakdowns. Technical Analysis tutorial.
https://www.YouTube.com/watch?v=GENBVwV8PMs

  SMA tutorial.
https://www.YouTube.com/watch?v=Na-ctpPsnks

Links

Fidelity video: Technical Analysis
https://www.fidelity.com/learning-center/technical-analysis/chart-types-video

Appendix 1   – All my books

- Complete the Art of Investing (highly recommended combining most of my books on investing). The Kindle version has over 850 pages (6*9).

- Sector Rotation: 21 Strategies (highly recommended for short-term investors) has more specific chapters on the topic and shares many articles with "Complete the art of investing".

- Best stocks for 2021. Not a promise: Another "Best stocks" books available on July, 2021 and Dec. 15, 2021.

- China: "Apocalypse or Co-prosperity (highly recommended). Trade War (most popular here) with China. Trade War & Pandemic. Rising China. Fall of an Empire: U.S.A. A Nation of No Losers. Can China Say No. Global Economies. Pandemic.

- Books for today's market: Profit from Coming Market Crash.

- The following books are in a series: Finding Profitable Stocks, Market Timing and Scoring Stocks. Alternate book Using Fidelity.com.

- Books on strategies: Shorting, "Profit from bull, bear and sideways markets" (Rotation + Momentum + ETF Rotation + trend following), Trading System (similar to printed version of Complete), Swing (Rotation + Momentum), ETF Rotation for Couch Potatoes, Momentum, SuperStocks, Dividend, Penny & Micro Stock, and Retiree.

- Books for advance beginners: Be an expert (highly recommended), Introduce . Billionaire (perfect gift for recent college graduates and they will thank you when they become millionaires), Investing for Beginners, Beat Fund Managers, Profit via ETFs, Buffett, Ideas, Conservative and Top-Down.
- Miscellaneous: Lessons in Investing. Investing Strategies. Buy Low and Sell High. Buy High and sell Higher. Buffettology. Technical Analysis. Trading Stocks.
- Concise Editions and Introduction Editions are available at very low prices and are competitive with books of similar sizes (50 pages) and prices ($3 range).

Most books have paperbacks. Links and offers are subject to change without notice.

Appendix 2 – Complete the Art of Investing

Instead of buying 16 books, why not buy one book (Complete the Art of Investing) consisting of 16 books? Besides saving money and your digital shelve space, it gives you quick reference and concentration on the topic you're currently interested in. It covers most investing topics in investing excluding speculative investing such as currency trading and day trading.

The Kindle version has about 850 pages (6*9), about the size of three books of average size. With the cost of $10 and at least 850 investing ideas, it is about one cent per idea. Most other books have only a few ideas in the entire book

The 16 books

This book "Complete Art of Investing" is divided into 16 books as follows. Click for the link to the book described in Amazon.com. I squeezed more than 3,000 pages into 850 pages by eliminating duplicated information such as evaluating stocks.

Book No.	Amazon.com
1	Beginner & Billionaire
2	Finding Stocks
3	Evaluating Stocks
4	Scoring Stocks
5	Trading Stocks
6	Market Timing
7	Strategies
8	Sector Rotation
9	Insider Trading
10	Penny Stocks & Micro Cap
11	Momentum Investing
12	Dividend Investing
13	Technical Analysis
14	Investing Ideas
15	The Economy
16	Buffettology

The book links are subject to change without notice.

"How to be a billionaire" is for beginners and couch potatoes, who can use the advanced features of this book in the simplest and less time-consuming techniques. Most advance users can skip this section unless they want to use some of the short cuts described.

We start with the basic books Finding Stocks, Evaluate Stocks, Trading Stocks and Market Timing. You can select and start with one of the many styles and strategies in investing such as swing trading and top-down strategy. Many tools are described in other books such as ETFs, technical analysis, covered calls and trading plan.

Many books start with "Why" to lure you to read more and are followed by "How" and then the theory behind the book.
If the book you're reading is beneficial to you, imagine how it would with 850 pages.

#

Most readers' comments are on "Debunk the Myths in Investing", which this book is originally based on.

"I skipped ahead to his chapter book 14 (of "Complete the Art of Investing"), Investment Advice just to get a feel of his writing style. His research is phenomenal and doesn't overwhelm with big words or catchy "sales-like"   tactics.

I truly believe this ordinary man, Mr. Tony Pow, has a gift of explaining his experience as an investor without the bull crap of trying to make you buy his stuff. He seemingly just wants to share his knowledge, tips, and clarity of definitions for the kind of folks like me who want to understand something FIRST before jumping in with emotions of trying to make a boat load of money. I like the technical analysis side he brings.

Mr. Tony Pow talks about hidden gems in his book; well....quite frankly, he is a hidden gem. Thank you and I will also post my comments about this author to my Facebook page!" – JB on this book.

"Excellent book, recommend to all investors... great knowledge. It has fine-tuned my investing strategies... Your book is hard to set aside, as I read it all the time learning good techniques and analysis of stocks, ETF... Since I purchased your book in March, I have underlined, highlighted and placed tabs on top of pages for quick reference." – Aileron on this book.

"Tony, I just finished reading your 2nd edition. It's my pleasure to report that I found it most interesting. You're welcome to use this blurb if you like:

Debunk the Myths in Investing is an all-encompassing look at not only the most salient factors influencing markets and investors, but also a from-the-trenches look at many of the misconceptions and mistakes too many investors make. Reading this book may save not only time and aggravation but money as well!"

Joseph Shaefer, CEO, Stanford Wealth Management LLC.

"Tony, Great work!" from James and Chris, who are portfolio managers.

"'Debunk the Myths in Investing' is a comprehensive book on investing that deals with many aspects of this tense profession in which with a lot of knowledge and a bit of luck (or vice versa) one can greatly benefit...

Therefore 'Debunk the Myths in Investing' is an interesting book that on its 500 pages offer a lot of knowledge related to investing world and many practical advice, so I can recommend its reading if you're interested in this topic."
- Denis Vukosav, Top 500 Reviewers at Amazon.com.

"490 pages (Debunk) of a genius's ranting and hypothesis with various theories throughout, written light-heartedly with ample doses of humor...Yes, the myth of not being able to profitably time the market is BUSTED...

One might ask... Why is he giving away the results of his hard-earned research for only $20? He states that his children are not interested in investing and wants to share his efforts with the world." - Abe Agoda.

"Excellent book, recommend to all investors... great knowledge. It has fine-tuned my investing strategies... Your book is hard to set aside, as I read it all the time learning good techniques and analysis of stocks, ETF... Since I purchased your book in March, I have underlined, highlighted and placed tabs on top of pages for quick reference." - Aileron on this book.

"Great stuff, Tony. It's great to meet experienced traders such as yourself. I had a browse through the book and think your method is a little more refined than mine."
"Your strategy is very rules based and solid. I sometimes envy people who have developed something like this."

Making 50% in one month
I claim to have the best one-month performance ever for recommending 8 or more stocks without using options and leverage. My following return is 57% in a month or 621% annualized. They are slightly different as I calculated the average from the averages of three different accounts. The average buy date is 12/26/18 and the "current date" is 01/28/19.

The performance may not be repeated. I will use the same screen for the coming years and even the expected 10% (or 120% annualized) is very good.

I used the same screen for searching stock candidates. I spent a total of about 20 hours from Dec. 15, 2018 to Jan. 5, 2019.

Stock	Buy Price	Sold or Current Price	Buy date	Sold or Current date	Profit %	Profit % Ann.	Status
CHK	2.13	2.99	01/03/09	01/18/19	40%	982%	Sold
MNK	16.41	21.45	01/03/19	01/25/19	31%	510%	Sold
MNK	16.43	21.45	01/03/19	01/25/19	31%	507%	Sold
NNBR	5.68	8.58	12/26/18	01/28/19	51%	565%	
NNBR	5.72	8.58	12/26/18	01/28/19	66%	727%	
ESTE	4.35	6.45	12/26/18	01/18/19	48%	766%	Sold
LCI	4.61	8.29	12/21/18	01/28/19	80%	767%	
MDR	8.01	9.13	01/08/19	01/28/19	14%	255%	
YRCW	3.29	5.78	12/21/18	01/28/19	76%	727%	
YRCW	3.26	5.78	12/21/18	01/28/19	77%	742%	
ASRT	3.56	4.18	12/26/18	01/28/19	17%	193%	
UTCC	7.13	11.00	12/26/18	01/28/19	54%	600%	
YRCW	2.92	5.78	12/26/18	01/28/19	98%	1083%	

Best one-year return
I claim to have the best-performed article in Seeking Alpha history, an investing site, for recommending 15 or more stocks in one year after the publish date without using options and leverage.

Your choice

"Complete the art of investing" should be your first choice. "Sector Rotation: 21 Strategies" and "Sell Short Stocks /ETFs" are your better choice depending on how often you rotate sectors or selling short. All three books share most articles. "Best Stocks" select the stocks for the period. "Be a stock expert in 5 minutes" and "Beat the fund managers" are books for beginner investors. "China and U.S." is my book on politics.

Sector Rotation: 21 Strategies

- On 5/26/2020, I searched for "Sector Rotation" under Amazon's Book. They are listed in the same order except my book Sector Rotation: 21 Strategies.

Book	Date	Size[1]	Kindle $[1]	Hard $
Sector Rotation: 21 Strategies	**05/2020**	**425**	**$9.95**	$24.95
Super Sectors	09/2010	289	$26.39	$49.95
Dual Momentum Investing	11/2014	240	$40.40	$42.20
Sector Investing	05/1996	260		$29.94
Sector Trading Strategies	08/2007	164	$26.39	$16.66
The Sector Strategist	03/2012	225	$26.39	$44.96
ETF Rotation	10/2012	125	**$9.95**	**$14.99**
Optimal... Sector Rotation	07/2015	80		$44.07

[1] From Amazon on size and prices as of 5/25/2020.

My book won in all categories except the price for hard copy in one. However, my book won as the lowest cost per page by a wide margin. In addition, as of 5/2020 I bet that no author besides me made over 4 times using sector rotation starting the amount more than his yearly salary then.

- I have **21** strategies in sector rotation while most books have only one. It ranges from simple rotation of a stock ETF and cash for beginners to many advanced strategies for experts. Most other books have one or two strategies.

- Andrew, a contributor on Sector Rotation article at Seeking Alpha, said, "Great stuff, Tony. It's great to meet experienced traders such as yourself. I had a browse through the book and think your method is a little more refined than mine."

- "You have written the book in a way that makes good and logical sense." Bill.
- Do not be fooled by past performances. Just check the recent performance of the top 50 stocks selected by IBD in the last five years. The mediocre result (hopefully it will change) could be due to too many followers and/or there is no evergreen strategy. I seldom heard the fantastic results from the followers of O'Neil, our greatest chartist. The adaptive strategy of this book shows you how to select the most profitable strategy for the current market.
- I switched most (if not all) my sector funds in April, 2000 from technology sectors to traditional sectors (better to money market fund). We can reduce losses by spotting market plunges and the sector trend.

My motivation to write this book is sharing my experiences, both bad and good. I provide simple-to-follow techniques using the free (or low-cost) resources available to us. I have been successful in investing for decades. I am enjoying a comfortable financial life. I do not hold back my 'secrets' as my children are not interested in investing. If you are looking how to make 100% return overnight, there are many other books claiming to do so and this book is not for you. This book describes how to be a 'turtle' investor making fortune gradually and surely. Be warned that many books written by authors who have never make money in the stock market.

Best stocks to buy for 2021

We care about performance only. The last book beats the market (SPY simulating S&P500 index) by 29%. Click here for the book or type the following for more info on the book.
https://www.amazon.com/dp/B08Q8R6SXQ

This is the performance of my last book "Best Stocks to buy from August, 2020". Past performances do NOT guarantee future performances.

The performance is the returns from 07/28/2020 to 12/07/2020. The average of the 14 recommended stocks beats SPY (an ETF simulating S&P500 stocks) by 29%. There are 13 winners and 1 loser. Dividends have not been included. CMCSA and FDX are big winners profiting from the pandemic.

Symbol	Name	Sector	True EY[1]	Return[2]	Ann. Return[2]
ABBV	AbbVie	Drug	7%	10%	27%
ABT	Abbott	Drug	3%	8%	21%
CHE	Chemed	Diversified	4%	4%	12%
CMCSA	Comcast	Media	11%	19%	52%
FDX	FedEx	Transport	8%	76%	211%
GTS	Triple-S	Health	N/A	26%	72%
JNJ	Jonson & J	Drug	6%	2%	4%
MCK	McKesson	Drug	8%	16%	45%
MSFT	Microsoft	Software	4%	6%	18%
SCHN	Schnitzer	Metal	10%	46%	127%
SMCI	Super Micro	Computer	11%	9%	24%
UFPI	Universal	Building	10%	-6%	-17%
UNH	United Health	Health	9%	15%	43%
ZBRA	Zebra Tech	Computer	5%	39%	107%
Avg.				19%	53%
		SPY		15%	41%
	Beat SPY by				**29%**

[1] True EY is the reciprocal of "EV/EBITDA". [2] Rounded up for easy reading, but not in the calculation in "Beat SPY by".

It is not a promise: I may have a similar book after 7/1 and 12/1 every year. Check my blog. https://tonyp4idea.blogspot.com/

Sell Short Stocks / ETFs

Book	Date	Size	Kindle $	Hard $
This book (Sell Short Stocks /ETFs)	**10/2020[1]**	**700[2]**	**$9.95**	**$26.95**
Short selling with the O'Neil Disciples	04/2015	336	$31.99	$43.22
The New sell & sell short	03/2011	368	$20.79	$31.57
Sell Short	03/2009	240	$18.39	$26.88
Sell and sell short	05/2008	250	N/A	$43.21

China and U.S: Apocalypse or Co-Prosperity

On 11/2020, I searched for "Trade War China" under Amazon's Book. They are listed in the same order except my book. This represents and summarizes most of my books on politics.

Book	Date	Size[1]	Kindle $[1]	Paper $
This book	**12/2020**	**428**	**$4.95**	**$14.95**
The U.S. – China Trade War: Conflict	**10/2020**	302	$9.95	**$14.99**
Us Vs China: From trade war...	09/2019	346	$11.59	$28.00
The China-US. Trade war and future economic relations	12/2018	222	$39.00	$39.00
Stealth War	10/2019	255	$7.95	$18.29

You have been brainwashed by our government and the media on China that has been demonized every day. I can say the same to the Chinese in China. My book is a summary of all my books on politics and hopefully represents the unbiased views from many overseas Chinese. That is why we have conflicts between the two countries.

Appendix 3 - Our window to the investing world

The paperback version of this chapter can be found in the following link.
http://ebmyth.blogspot.com/2013/11/web-sites.html

- **General**
  Wikipedia / Investopedia /Yahoo!Finance / MarketWatch / Cnnfn / Morningstar /CNBC / Bloomberg / WSJ / Barron's / Motley Fool / TheStreet
- **Evaluate stocks**
  Finviz / SeekingAlpha / MSN Money / Zacks / Daily Finance / ADR / Fidelity / BlueChipGrowth / Earnings Impact / OpenInsider / NYSE / NASDAQ / SEC / SEC for 10K and 10Q (quarterly) reports required to file for listed stocks in major exchanges.
- **Charts**
  BigCharts / FreeStockCharts / StockCharts /
- **Screens**
  Yahoo!Finance / Finviz / CNBC / Morningstar /
- **Besides stocks**
  123Jump / Hoover's Online / FINRA Bond Market Data / REIT / Commodity Futures / Option Industry
- **Vendors**
  AAII / Zacks / IBD / GuruFocus / Vector Vest / Fidelity / Interactive Brokers / Merrill Lynch /
- **Economy.**
  Econday / EcoconStats / Federal Reserve / Economist /
- **Misc.**
  Dow Jones Indices / Russell / Wilshire / IRS / Wikinvest / ETF Database / ETF Trends / Nolo (estate planning) / AARP /

#Filler: Honey, my book can play music.

https://www.youtube.com/watch?v=HxGT5z6d-GA&list=PLMZa6mP7jZ2b1otqG4tfbgZpLEdh6YiNF

It may cut down commercials by casting it to TV.

www.ingramcontent.com/pod-product-compliance
Lightning Source LLC
Chambersburg PA
CBHW070933180526
45168CB00003B/1056